# Praise for *Please Explain "Time Out" To Me*

Drs. Zelinger have given a true gift to parents and their children with this book. While clearly informed by literature and both clinical and personal experience, its simplicity and ease-of-use and understanding allows for a broad reach to all parents that face the normal challenges in raising children. What makes this book even more special and unique is the story to aid understanding of the child, as well as the "fixer box" concept. Behavioral difficulties often stem from struggles around feeling in control. This book gives a concrete, more adaptive path for both parents and child to feel in control.

David Salsberg, PsyD, DABPS Clinical Neuropsychologist; Director, Pediatric Assessment, Learning & Support (PALS), New York, NY.

In *Please Explain Time Out to Me,* Drs. Laurie and Fred Zelinger offer a clear, concise and insightful look at the often misunderstood and misinterpreted concept of Time Out. Combining colorful illustrations and a storyline for children, as well as step-by-step guidelines and principles for parents and adults, the book has unique appeal to both. Drawing on years of professional expertise and personal experience, the Zelingers characteristically share their knowledge in sensible familiar language that is relatable, wise and compassionate. I highly recommend this book, particularly to parents foraging through the tangled, complicated and sometimes scary web called parenthood.

Iris Ackerman, LCSW, PhD, Clinical Social Worker

The Drs. Zelinger have created a combination guide for children and parents that is a practical, respectful and sensible approach to discipline. The child's predicament is made very clear and parents are guided with practical steps for a positive outcome. Characters represent diversity and come to life with vivid illustrations and recognizable scenarios. Children will find the storyline engaging, while the parent section provides valuable information regarding positive and negative consequences in the management of behavior.

Stephanie Rosen, RN

*Please Explain Time Out To Me* provides a useful, child-friendly explanation of the handy and gentle Time Out procedure. When done properly, Time Out can be a very effective addition to our parenting toolbox.

Thomas W. Phelan, PhD, Psychologist, Author *1-2-3 Magic*

As a child psychiatrist, finding parenting books that are straightforward, helpful and concise is a rare find, indeed. Drs. Laurie and Fred Zelinger offer just that in *Please Explain Time Out To Me*. In its pages, they harness their expert clinical experience and judgment and offer it in a relatable, engaging and entertaining way. I highly recommend this book to families who are struggling with the difficult journey of growing up and managing problem behaviors along the way.

Stephen Perret, MD., Child Psychiatrist

Thumbs up for Drs. Zelinger's book on explaining Time Out to kids. As a busy working mom with six children, I have used Time Out effectively. I would recommend reading this book to help understand the benefits of Time Out for both parents and children, and the effectiveness of time-out as a learning tool. Drs. Zelinger's thought out story will be a helpful, useful contribution for kids, parents and teachers.

Chani Jacobowitz, LCSW; Mother of 6

*Please Explain Time Out To Me* is an excellent book for both children and parents. Parents are given an excellent way to explain Time Out to their children and children can listen to or read the rationale of this method of behavior modification. The book's text and illustrations will lead to healthy, non-threatening child-parent conversations.

Lydia A. Parris, Retired Principal Long Beach, NY;
Coordinator, Educational Administration Program,
College of St. Rose/Center for Integrated Teacher Education

# Please Explain "Time Out" To Me:

## A Story for Children and Do-It-Yourself Manual for Parents

## By Laurie Zelinger, Ph.D., ABPP, RPT-S and Fred Zelinger, Ph.D.

Loving Healing Press
Ann Arbor, MI

Look for audiobook editions of all of Laurie Zelinger's works in the "Please Explain" series at Audible.com, Amazon, and iTunes stores.

Learn more at www.DrZelinger.com

| Library of Congress Cataloging-in-Publication Data |
| --- |
| Names: Zelinger, Laurie E., 1952- author. \| Zelinger, Fred, 1949- author.<br>Title: Please explain "time out" to me : a story for children and do-it-yourself manual for parents / Dr. Laurie Zelinger and Dr. Fred Zelinger.<br>Description: Ann Arbor, MI : Loving Healing Press, [2018] \| Includes bibliographical references. \| Audience: Ages 5-9. \| Audience: Grades K-3.<br>Identifiers: LCCN 2018040237\| ISBN 9781615994151 (pbk. : alk. paper) \| ISBN 9781615994168 (hardcover : alk. paper)<br>Subjects: LCSH: Behavior modification--Juvenile literature. \| Timeout method--Juvenile literature.<br>Classification: LCC BF637.B4 .Z45 2018 \| DDC 153.8/5--dc23<br>LC record available at https://lccn.loc.gov/2018040237 |

Published by
Loving Healing Press
5145 Pontiac Trail
Ann Arbor, MI 48105

www.LHPress.com
info@LHPress.com
Tollfree (USA/CA) 888-761-6268
FAX 734-663-6861

# Contents

## Dedication

This book is dedicated to Laurie's brother David, who when he was young and at the edge of mischief, promised their father that he was indeed "being haved." It is also lovingly dedicated to our sons, who gave us plenty of opportunity to practice using Time Out.

# Introduction (for Parents only)

Parent training begins the moment we are born and continues over our lifetime. Our own parents were our first teachers and our children are the next generation of instructors, furthering our education and molding our roles as teachers of discipline, organization, planning and emotional self-regulation. With all these years of training, it is often surprising how many dilemmas, poor decisions and confusion we experience as our parenting skills repeatedly get tested. Raising children can certainly be complicated. We want our children to evolve into independent, kindhearted social beings, who are comfortable with themselves and others; attainable when environments are loving and filled with praise. We teach our children to live within the rules of the world and we correct their behavior when they stray. Giving advance thought to the parenting process, determining one's beliefs regarding rewards and consequences, and indulging in regular re-evaluation of the success of our chosen approaches are important aspects of effective parenting.

The scope of parenting is so vast, however, that we have chosen to focus primarily on the popular discipline technique known as, "Time Out From Reinforcement," or as known by its more common name, simply, "Time Out." Time Out has acquired a number of definitions over the years, most of which are well regarded, and supported by the American Psychological Association and the American Academy of Pediatrics. In the New York Times article, "Timeouts for Everyone" (April 2, 2019), Time Out has once again been identified as an effective discipline model of choice for young children. Although some opponents have suggested that the process engenders possible feelings of shame within the child, we are proposing a love-based model of parent discipline where Time Out is redefined as a caring establishment of boundaries, and children participate in discussion regarding its purpose, duration, location and criteria for use in advance. As in sports, the phrase "Time Out" has been popularized to mean a pause in the action allowing for reflection, regrouping, and redirection of behavior, and provides structure when children need to reset. As experienced psychologists, parents, and grandparents, we have found remarkable success when Time Out is used correctly and with dignity. We have created this book for two different audiences by offering an engaging, colorful story for children and a do-it-yourself manual for parents.

The children's story, filled with colorful illustrations, will resonate with any child who has ever misbehaved. Kids will identify with the character's frustrations, boredom, anger and feelings as he sits in Time Out. The section for parents contains a 'how-to" guide, as well as detailed explanations of various consequences. Because some of the information is rather technical, the reader may opt to skim those sections and return for an in-depth reading at a later date. For caregivers hoping for a more comprehensive tutorial, however, the section, "Scientifically Speaking" should meet their needs. Our suggestion is that parents thoroughly read both the child and parent portions of this book before creating any change in discipline practices.

We have learned that parenting is retrospective. Examining our mistakes teaches us what has worked and what hasn't, providing the information for us to do it better next time (and if you have children, there will always be a next time!) Both our conscious and unconscious feelings about parenting can best be understood by looking back. In keeping with this concept, our book starts in the back for parents, and in the front for children. We hope you find it to be a helpful resource.

Drs. Laurie and Fred Zelinger
Clinical Psychologists

Hi. My name is Jackson and I have an older stepsister, a younger brother named Liam, a dog named Max, and a fish named Dragon. I like some sports, video games, sushi, building stuff, and playing. I don't like homework, brushing my teeth, doing chores, or waiting for things I want. But most of the time I'm good.

This is my bedroom. This is where I keep everything important to me and secret stuff I don't want anyone to touch. When I used to misbehave, I got sent to my room. That was okay with me because Dragon and I like it there and there were plenty of things to do.

So, listen to what happened yesterday in school. We were lining up for recess and I could hardly wait to go on the monkey bars. All of a sudden, Lucas cut in front of me and I got so mad! I pushed him out of the way and he fell down and started to cry. The teacher sent him to the nurse and sent me to the Vacation Station spot, the seat in the back of the room where kids go when they need to think about their behavior. It didn't feel like vacation. No way. I like going to my room much better.

When I got home from school, Mom asked me, "How was school today?" I said, "Fine" and I hoped she wouldn't find out about recess.

The next day at school was pretty good. I did my best to follow the rules and I felt proud when my teacher told me she liked how I was keeping my hands to myself. The Vacation Station seat stayed empty all day.

After school, I was feeling happy and was even nice to little brother. I let him play with my Legos. Mom called me a lot of words I hadn't heard in a long time, like "kind," "helpful," "thoughtful," and "caring." Yep, most of the time, I'm good.

Finally, the weekend came. I was so excited because I didn't have to wake up early and brush my teeth. I fed Dragon, played with my Legos, and built an amazing tower that was taller than I am, even when I stand on my tiptoes. I could hardly wait for Mom to wake up to show her.

My brother woke up first and was calling me, but I tried to ignore him. He found me and my tower and wanted to help, but I just wanted him to go away. We started fighting, and in one second, he smashed my tower! It was ruined! I was madder than the time I almost exploded at the amusement park because the man said I wasn't tall enough to ride the Double Dipper, Go-Up Throw-Up, Upside Down, Spin Around, Faster Blaster ride. At that exact second, I could not control my hands. They just wanted to get back at Liam and make him cry.

Mom heard us both yelling and put us in Time Out. But in different places. Liam had a shorter time than I did because he's younger. I wish I was him. I had to sit in a chair facing the back of the bathroom door so that there was nothing good to look at to distract me, and Liam sat facing a boring wall. Mom went into the kitchen. I could hear her making breakfast, but she didn't ask us if we were hungry. In fact, she was barely even talking to us.

After a little while, Mom called out to me, "Three more minutes, Jackson!" but Liam was already done with his Time Out. He went to find her in the kitchen, and I heard her say she didn't feel like talking to him right now. Three more minutes was taking a really long time. I wanted to be in the kitchen, too, to see what was cooking.

Mom finally came over to me and asked if I was ready to come out of Time Out. I knew if I said, "No," I'd have to sit there for even longer. So I said, "Yes," which meant I had to show better behavior. I was finally allowed to leave the Time Out chair, and so I did, because I wanted to see what was going on. Frozen waffles were in the toaster. I said, "Thanks" to Mom, but she just said, "You're welcome" and nothing else.

Mom went to put clothes in the washing machine. I followed her there, but she wasn't in a talking mood. Then I followed her to the living room. And I even followed her to the bedroom. I was using my nicest indoor voice, but she still didn't feel like talking. I did not like Mom this way one little bit.

A few minutes later when Mom talked to me again, she told me how disappointed she was in my behavior. I felt better when she said she knew how hard I worked on building my tower and how upset it got me when Liam ruined it. We talked about things I could do the next time I get boiling mad instead of trying to get even. Then she said, "Okay let's start over and have a great day."

We ate waffles and got dressed because we had a lot to do. The weekend was sort of good because I had a soccer game and almost scored a goal. But the weekend was also sort of bad because I had to go to my brother's baseball practice and my sister's cheerleading practice, and there was nothing for me to do at either one. They were so boring and took so long. I hate waiting.

When we got home, there was nobody around to play with. I still had nothing to do. Liam had a playdate, and my sister was studying for a test. I asked if I could play on her phone and she kept saying no. After about the ninetieth time I asked, she told Mom that I was being annoying. Mom suggested I go to my room. Wait, what? Am I being punished? Mom said no, l didn't do anything wrong, but that I looked angry—like I needed to calm down, and my room was a good, comfy place to do that.

Mom wanted me to feel better and thought that maybe talking to Dragon would help. Since I like my room and it has things for me to do, she said I might be able to entertain myself. Going there to chill out and relax is *not* the same as being in a lonely and boring Time Out for breaking a rule. Now l I get it. This wasn't a consequence. Because most of the time I'm good.

I took out the special Frustration Fixer box that Dad and I had made. We decided to put things in it that I could use when I'm really mad or frustrated. (Turn to page 26 to see what I put in my box, but you can decide what to put in yours.) Since I usually feel the tension in my mouth and my hands, I chose things to help get out the mad energy. When I felt better, I went to apologize to my sister for the phone thing. It wasn't her problem that I was bored. I just hate waiting for things I want.

I behaved great for a long time after that and got special privileges because Mom and my teacher both said I was being responsible. Like I said, most of the time I'm good. But of course, I am a regular kid you know, and sometimes I get mad. Like when my parents tell me we're going to the park and we don't go. Or when my friend is busy and can't come over. Or when I want to eat junk food or buy something really cool and Mom says, "No." That's when I have to come up with something better than yelling and throwing things to get my feelings out.

Sometimes I try to "Stop and Think," count to ten, take slow, deep breaths, or punch my pillow. Sometimes I distract myself and try to think of something else. I know how to do wall push-ups and jumping jacks, but sometimes I like to make mean faces and growl instead.

I remember one time when I broke a major rule at home and Mom rushed me into Time Out so fast it felt like a hurricane in my house. I knew it was not going to be good. *Nah-uh*. I sat in that chair apart from everyone while they were lucky and got to watch a video. I heard them laughing and it made me jealous. I kept yelling for everyone to be quiet, but they just ignored me. Everyone knows the rule: Don't pay attention to anyone in Time Out until they come out! Ugh!

While I sat there in that boring chair, I thought about my behavior and realized it wasn't good. I wish I could go back and undo it. I didn't feel any better while I was misbehaving, and it felt like the whole world got mad at me. I was pretty embarrassed when I thought about what I had done. Besides, I missed out on some of the video, and they weren't going to rewind it for me. I was ready to try following the rules again.

I used to have to go into Time Out a lot more, but now I'm better at controlling my feelings and talking about what upsets me. If I can't figure it out, I ask for help or go into my room to try to calm down.

I like myself better when I'm not making a scene, having a meltdown or "having a tantrum," as my parents call it. Even though I don't like waiting, or hearing the word, "No" when I want something, I'm trying not to get upset since in real life, I can't get everything I want. Nobody can.

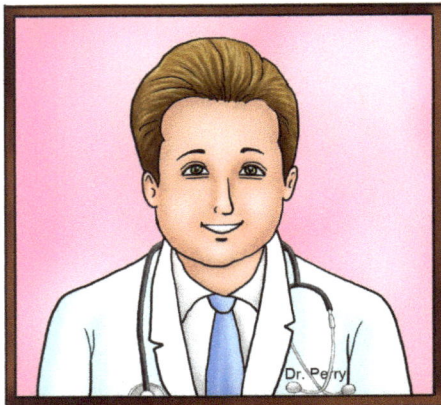

I don't recommend breaking rules that will get you put in Time Out, but it's a lot better than other kinds of consequences. Parents aren't allowed to do some kinds of punishment, and if they get carried away, you can tell your teacher or another grownup you trust. They will call special people to check it out because it is their job to protect kids.

Time Out kind of stinks, but you won't need it if you follow the rules. Once in a while, I make a mistake, and then I think about how to do better next time. Time Out lets me practice getting back in control so I can feel better and get back on track. It helps me remember what not to do and what I should do instead. I'm glad I don't need Time Out very much anymore. I'm proud to say, most of the time I'm good.

## My Frustration Fixer Box has these things:

- Bubbles to blow to help me calm down

- Kazoo to buzz into when I want to show everyone how mad I am

- Hard gum to chew

- Stretchy band to pull on

- A picture of me smiling to remind me that I'll feel better when this feeling goes away

- Bongo drum to hit

- Joke book

- Something squishy to squeeze

- A soft cloth that smells like lavender

- Pad and pencil to write down anything I want to remember or can't say out loud

- A toy lion to growl at

- A Transformer to remind me that I can change too

- Tissues in case I cry a lot

# Parent Guide to Effective Behavioral Management

According to the **American Academy of Pediatrics**: "Giving a child time-out can be a useful tool to help them cool down and learn good behavior."

*How to Give a Time Out* (updated Nov. 5, 2018)

## Introduction

If you are an adult living with a child, you have undoubtedly experienced the highs and lows of parenting. It is easy to be around children when they are at their best, but when their behavior signals an impending volcanic eruption, we need to step in and parent more actively. During those moments, our goal is usually to interrupt the behavior, restore calm, and provide opportunities for reflection, and the learning of better behaviors. It should also be our goal to remain clear-headed when responding to a child who needs our help. In the experience of these psychologists, parental rage is a common pitfall that adults experience when invoking a consequence. Parental anger at misbehavior is understandable and should be a reminder to think through one's goals. When you are angry with your child, it can lead to arguing, lecturing, fighting, or further escalation of emotions, none of which is effective in teaching a child to behave appropriately. Even more important, it provides a harmful model on how to react. Rather, having a discipline plan in mind that you believe in and to which you are committed, and delivering the selected consequence in a thoughtful, controlled manner will improve parental effectiveness. In contrast, parenting in the absence of a plan increases the likelihood that we fall victim to our own impulses and emotionality. Effective parenting is not a function of harshness or anger but rather of warmth, consistency and predictability. Think rationally, not emotionally, when intervention is necessary. But think emotionally and lovingly when it comes to praising your children and giving them positive messages.

The reader should be especially aware that these approaches can only be effective in the presence of an environment where children experience an ample supply of praise and appreciation rather than criticism. It is not the consequence alone that is working, but rather the juxtaposition of the child's remorseful feelings within the usual context of feeling comfortable. The contrast of these dichotomous feelings is responsible for how effective the approach is with the child.

## Changing a Behavior

It is believed by many professionals that what follows a behavior either leads to its increase or decrease. For example, if you worked hard to create a great meal and it met with rave reviews, you would likely want to serve it more often. However, if your family described it as "totally gross" and refused to eat it, you would not be likely to prepare that same meal in the future. The same thing happens with other forms of behavior. When we show children praise and appreciation of something, they are likely to repeat the behavior we are admiring. That is referred to as **positive reinforcement,** and it is unanimously regarded as the preferred method of maintaining or developing a desired behavior.

On the other hand, when our children show us those behaviors that turn our hair gray, we need to respond with an appropriate consequence. It is in everyone's best interests to use the least punitive method to accomplish our goal. Harsh is not better. It is not our goal to shame, anger, harm or scare a child. It is our goal to help them stop the objectionable behavior and to teach replacement behaviors in order that similar scenes do not recur. So, what should we do?

There is a science to encouraging good behavior. When we want to reduce the frequency or intensity of a behavior, we can either try to weaken it, or identify an acceptable competing behavior and work to increase that one. Even though many of our reactions may seem like natural and logical responses, we are using principles that have strong scientific backing.

Some confusion exists about rewards and punishment, and often parents tend to use the same methods of discipline used by their families when they were children, even if they don't work. When parenting without a plan, we fall victim to our own impulses, histories and emotions.

Parents should be aware of a hierarchy of consequences, with the least severe option being the first one chosen. While many adults have endured harsh physical punishments as children and report that they "turned out okay," many painful and humiliating forms of punishment are considered inappropriate or possibly even abusive by today's standards and have been replaced by effective methods of behavioral change that do not involve physical contact.

## Scientifically speaking...

**Positive reinforcement** ( ★ ★ ★ ★ ) is the term used to describe the pleasant action or thing that follows a behavior and strengthens it. If we like what we see in our child and we want to see more of it, we will respond with something that the child likes. For example, if a youngster seeks parent approval, our smile, hug, or words of praise will be a positive reinforcement. For children who respond to tangibles, treats or special activities could be selected. Reinforcers should be delivered immediately, and are subjective and very individualistic; what may be motivating to one child may not work for another. Positive reinforcement, when used judiciously upon the demonstration of a desired behavior, becomes a powerful tool in the process of change.

When positive reinforcement successfully strengthens a desired behavior, the non-desired behavior tends to weaken because two competing behaviors cannot occur at the same time. For example, a child cannot be punching somebody at the same time he is holding hands. If we want hitting to stop, we praise him for using gentle or "friendly hands" when playing with others or accomplishing something purposeful such as getting dressed, carrying objects, or sharing toys. Reinforcing comments should be specific and could begin with, "I like the way your hands are" (e.g., using your fork…passing the toy to your sister…helping your friend with his work, etc.).

**Positive reinforcement gets four stars!**

**Negative punishment** ( ✮ ✮ ✮ ) sounds bad but really is next in line in terms of preferred strategies. This means you are removing something the child likes following a behavior you do not like. For instance, if your child was surfing the internet without your permission, you would remove computer and television privileges. When you choose to take away TV or computer time, make sure you can supervise your child for the entire time you designate. Many savvy children have found a way to use these devices without their parents realizing it. Having the "punishment fit the crime" makes sense; the consequence should be relevant to the infraction and something you can realistically implement. Grounding a child and using Time Out are both forms of negative punishment because you are removing or separating the child from the excitement of the world around him. If you opt for Time Out, this is the only consequence needed. No additional consequences should be considered. Parents often question how long Time Out should last. Many experts recommend one minute for every year of age, whereby a 6-year-old would get 6 minutes. However, young children do not have an accurate sense of time since time is among the last of the basic concepts to be acquired before age five. As such, it is our belief that length of time in Time Out doesn't have to be a hard and fast rule and that each family should evaluate its own needs. It has been the experience of these psychologists that shorter, more frequent Time Outs can provide more practice opportunities from which to learn where even a few seconds of time might accomplish the goal.

Advantages to Time Out are numerous. It eliminates considerable yelling on the part of the parents, it is a consistent consequence that the child comes to expect based on previous discussions, the child learns to differentiate acceptable from unacceptable behaviors, the child learns self-control and self-soothing leading to a return of rational thinking, and the number of Time Outs used can be counted in order to determine the course of behavioral change.

**Negative punishment gets three stars!**

One issue that confuses parents is how to address behavior problems occurring in school. The question presents itself as, "Should I provide home consequences in support of school consequences, or should a consequence be limited to the environment in which the behavior occurs?" When a child breaks school rules, a school consequence is usually imposed based upon school policy (this is often detailed in your child's school handbook). Imagine the thoughts going through a child's mind as he wonders what will happen when he gets home. When your child comes off the school bus, he knows a reaction awaits him. Assuming that the school has addressed the situation, your cool demeanor will be consequence enough. These psychologists believe that an expression of parental concern and disapproval represents an appropriate home consequence when the infraction has already been dealt with at a school level. Clearly, if school misbehavior becomes an ongoing issue, the development of a more targeted plan may be indicated. School professionals can be helpful in this area and will advise you whether additional professional support is recommended at home. Regardless of how you feel as a parent, it is important not to position yourself as being critical of your child's school or teacher. If you do not agree with the handling of the issue, that should become an adult discussion.

\***Negative reinforcement** (*no stars*) occurs when a response is made stronger due to the removal of an unpleasant stimulus. Take this example. You are in a store with your child and he asks for a toy. You say, "No." He asks again. You say, "No" again. He begins to cry, yet you remain firm. He finally throws a tantrum, makes a scene, and embarrasses you, so you give in to make it stop. Congratulations! You have successfully taught your child to throw a tantrum in order to get what he wants. You have now experienced Negative Reinforcement for yourself first hand! You removed an unpleasant stimulus (his noise) and strengthened his behavior because he upped his game, and he now knows exactly what to do next time he wants a toy. Although your child didn't experience negative reinforcement, you did.

*Tip: Practice saying, "No," and mean it, or bring plenty of extra cash to the store next time.*
Negative reinforcement is a tricky concept and has little real-life application, since deliberately supplying an unpleasant or painful stimulus to our children is not recommended.
**Negative Reinforcement gets no stars!**

**Positive punishment (including corporal punishment):** This form of discipline has the potential to be the harshest and most uncompassionate. It is recognized that cultures vary in their beliefs; but our goal as caregivers should be to love, protect, and teach our children in the most caring way possible. While yelling is the mildest form of Positive Punishment and is often ineffective, cursing at a child is unacceptable. It is never okay to lock children outside or in dark places, beat them with belts or objects, cause injury, withhold nourishment, or put soap in their mouths. Child Protective Services can intervene for punishments such as these. If parents feel so frustrated that they cannot summon rational alternatives, they should seek support from someone they trust. Besides, aggression breeds aggression. The **American Professional Society on the Abuse of Children** (APSAC) specifically states:

> Young children who experience corporal punishment are at greater risk for Child Protective Services involvement. Additionally, corporal punishment is related to a host of negative outcomes for children, including risk for child behavioral problems such as increased aggression and antisocial behavior. No studies show that corporal punishment has positive effects on children or leads to improved child behavior. (July 26, 2016)

**American Psychological Association** "Resolution on Physical Discipline of Children by Parents" advises:

> …there is no consistent scientific evidence that physical discipline makes children more or less likely to cease undesirable behavior or engage in desirable behavior in the short term (Gershoff & Grogan-Kaylor, 2016a). Research instead suggests that physical discipline is not better than other discipline methods (e.g., reasoning, time out, taking away privileges, warnings, and ignoring misbehavior) nor does it serve to enhance the positive outcomes parents seek, such as conscience development or positive behavior and affect (Larzelere & Kuhn, 2005). Instead, use of physical discipline predicts increases—not

decreases—in children's behavior problems over time, even after race, gender, and family socioeconomic status have been statistically controlled. (February 15, 2019)

**Positive Punishment gets no stars!**

**Natural Consequences:** While many options for reinforcement can be manipulated by us, others occur naturally within the child's world without our help. Natural consequences refer to the feedback from others that occur without any planned intervention on our part. For example, if our child was bossy to her friend during a playdate, the friend might decide not to come over again. Or if we sent a tuna fish sandwich in for lunch and her friends said it smelled disgusting, our child would probably opt out of tuna fish for the remainder of the year. Natural consequences are the reactions of others that change the trajectory of future behaviors. They are powerful, and have lasting effects.

## Walk the Walk

Effective parenting is about believing in what you do—not just doing it. For healthy emotional development, it is important to establish boundaries in order to help children understand limits. "No" is an act of love, and contrary to what your child might tell you, not a function of being "mean." The alignment between our thoughts and practices is what creates the type of parenting and teaching that children trust and respond to. Children feel safe when adults are in charge.

Some aspect of children's need to test limits, push against boundaries, or oppose our rules is built into the developmental process as a way of learning about their world. This type of investigation is needed for healthy growth and should be supported by parents, while also ensuring that we wisely maintain boundaries and sustain our ability to say "No." Children make mistakes, and often those mistakes can become teachable moments without criticism or need for a consequence. When a child engages in unacceptable, harmful, or dangerous action that impacts health or safety, however, that behavior must be stopped quickly, firmly, and decisively. The least intrusive consequence that works should always be used first. Severe consequences should be reserved only for severe events when a lesser response would not be effective.

Consequences should be immediate, firm, and consistent. A behavior that is severe enough to warrant a consequence at any time should receive a consequence every time it occurs. You need to have a plan in place.

## Tricky Situations

Our children are constantly presenting us with good and bad situations that require us to take some sort of action. The authors are sympathetic to the difficulty parents have when implementing behavior management strategies, given the complexities of real life. The presence of several children within a family, misbehavior that occurs when you are not home, the effect of having two homes following divorce, or the inclusion of babysitters and other caregivers in a child's life can make the teaching of appropriate behavior even more complicated. Children are required to understand expectations, rules, and consequences in multiple settings. While they are capable of differentiating what is expected in each setting, alignment between and among environments will facilitate implementation of any plan. When one setting is lenient and another strict, children will be more likely to test limits and see what they can get away with.

Tricky situations do not always allow an optimal response, but a good faith effort should be made as quickly and as feasibly as possible given the circumstances. For example, when a child breaks a rule in the supermarket, Time Out should be implemented as soon as possible. If necessary, immediately leave the store and give your child Time Out in the car. You can return to the store as soon as he reestablishes control. Don't worry about feeling embarrassed. Every parent can identify with you.

If you are at a friend's house, implement the same procedure you would at home. If it happens in the car, such as when a child is dangerously interfering with your driving, pull over and have the child remain in his seat while you and your other children exit the car and stand safely within view until the time is over. In the case of divorce, the two parent homes are not expected to be identical in practice, but when the underlying principles of management are in agreement, greater likelihood exists that effective management practices will prevail. When expectations are consistent, children accept them more readily.

## Time Out: 5 Essential Steps

1. **In advance and as a family, identify why, when, how and where Time Out will be implemented.** Make sure that all children understand its purpose and the behaviors that will result in Time Out. Choose a location in your home away from most of the action, where there is as little stimulation as possible, and where a chair is easily accessible so that your child can be comfortable. Remember, "Time Out" is Time Out from positive Reinforcement, and anything that captures your child's interest has the potential to be reinforcing, so the plainest location is the most desirable (i.e., near a closed door or blank wall). Have a designated spot on each floor of your home as the Time Out location since you will want to keep the child within your vision throughout the process. The idea is not to frighten a child who may not want to be left alone, and it is not about isolation. Rather, it is merely to remove children from the reinforcers that usually surround them. Many parents send children to their rooms for Time Out. The problem with this is twofold: rooms are usually full of stimulation, and so your goal will not be accomplished. Second, any child with sleep issues might come to associate the bedroom with reprimand, thereby contributing to more resistance at bedtime. Other parents choose to remove their child but send him or her to sit on the stairs. While their intent may be good, this perch provides the child with a good overview of the house, much like a supervisor surveying the action, rather than a child who is supposed to be separated from the action and unable to participate.

2. **If a rule has been broken that cannot be corrected by discussion, *swiftly* move or carry your child to the Time Out Chair.** Identify in as few, crisp words as possible, the rule that has been broken (i.e. "No biting!" "No throwing toys!" "No hurting sister!"). Deposit your child in the Time Out chair and walk away. Do not answer his or her questions or have any discussion except to announce how much more time the child has left in Time Out. If your daughter comes out of Time Out prematurely, walk her back. If she refuses to remain there or begins wiggling out, keep your hands on her shoulders for as long as necessary while she sits in the chair. Do not speak to her. When the designated time has been reached, you can ask, "Are you ready to come out?" If she says "Yes," you can walk away. If she continues to scream, you might say, "It seems as though you are not ready yet. You need a few more minutes," and repeat the sequence. If your child absolutely will not stay in Time Out, you can symbolically create the Time Out in the room where the child's behavior occurred by removing yourself. While not optimal, it is a possible alternative

3. **When one child is in Time Out, the whole world doesn't have to stop.** It is all right to carry on activities with your other children, but you would not want your separated child to enjoy listening to the television program that his siblings might be watching. Feeling left out of the action is what drives the change in behavior. If your child does not like being in Time Out, she will be more likely to show compliant behavior to avoid it in the future.

4. **When Time Out is over, you should go about your business without any further discussion with this child.** He will likely follow you around because he wants to restore the relationship. At that point you might say that you are happy to see he has calmed down, but that you need a few more seconds. The absence of a connection to you is by itself a powerful form of consequence, so it should be used judiciously and for the briefest time. This provides the child with an opportunity to establish a relationship between his behavior and the feelings of others, thereby creating a better understanding of empathy.

5. **After a few seconds or minutes have elapsed, you can approach your child** and discuss what went wrong and how you were disappointed in his choices but that you can help him find ways to better express his negative feelings next time. You have now completed the Time Out process, can reset, and return to all previous activities.

## Conclusion

While the ideas and principles behind Time Out appear simple and straightforward, they must be adapted and utilized to suit your family's dynamics. Parenting is a process that requires close attention and active participation in order to raise physically and emotionally healthy children. Fortunately, if you feel you didn't handle a situation as well as you would have liked at some point, the long term process of parenting pretty much guarantees that you will have plenty of opportunities to do it better next time. Perseverance, self-reflection, and recognition of parenting as a process—not an event—will go a long way to establishing an effective approach to parenting.

## Glossary

**Reinforcement**: Something that follows a behavior and increases its rate of occurrence. Reinforcements strengthen the tendency of responding.

**Positive reinforcement**: A response is strengthened because it is followed by something pleasant.

**Negative reinforcement**: A response is strengthened because it is followed by the removal of a (presumably) unpleasant stimulus.

**Intermittent reinforcement** (either positive or negative): occurs when reinforcement follows a particular response only some of the time and not after every occurrence. When this type of reinforcement is used, it tends to make it harder to end a behavior because the child will usually continue to engage in the behavior, expecting that at some point, a reinforcer will be delivered.

**Punishment** occurs when a behavior is weakened based upon the response that immediately follows it.

**Positive punishment**: A response is followed by the presentation of an aversive or harsh stimulus (i.e., yelling at or spanking, being placed in a dark or locked area). While spanking may temporarily reduce a behavior, the long-term effects lean toward increasing aggression in the child.

**Negative punishment**: A response is weakened because it is followed by the removal of something the child likes (i.e., watching TV, playing video games, riding his bicycle). Time Out is an example of negative punishment because the child is removed from the activities he enjoys.

⭐⭐⭐⭐ **4 STARS!**      ⭐⭐⭐ **3 STARS!**      **0 STARS!**

| POSITIVE REINFORCEMENT: A behavior is strengthened because it is followed by something pleasant. | NEGATIVE PUNISHMENT An objectionable behavior is weakened by removing something the child likes. | NEGATIVE REINFORCEMENT: A behavior is strengthened by removing something unpleasant. |
|---|---|---|
| | | POSITIVE PUNISHMENT: A harsh punishment is applied following a behavior you want to weaken. |

## Other Time Out Books for Children

Cartwright, Susan (2018). *The time out chair*. USA: Christian Faith Publishing, Inc.

Mayer, Kally (2015). *Gross Gus and the time out chair*. USA: Picture Perfect Publishing

Moua, Vinai (2016). *Timeout STINKS!* USA: Amazon Digital Services, LLC

Nelsen, Jane (2013). *Jared's cool-out space*. Orem, Utah: Positive Discipline

Nicholson, Shelly. (2009) *Jake the snake and the stupid time-out chair*. Baltimore: PublishAmerica

# About the Authors

**Dr. Laurie Zelinger** is a Board Certified Psychologist with a specialty in School Psychology, and a Registered Play Therapist with over 40 years' experience working with children. She is a licensed New York State psychologist who, after retiring from a Long Island public school system, is now devoting her time exclusively to writing and her busy private practice. Her previous books include: *Please Explain Anxiety to Me: Simple Biology and Solutions for Children and Parents*; *Please Explain Tonsillectomy & Adenoidectomy to Me: A Complete Guide to Preparing Your Child for Surgery*; *Please Explain Terrorism to Me! A Story for Children, P-E-A-R-L-S of Wisdom for Their Parents* and *A Smart Girl's Guide to Liking Herself Even On The Bad Days* for American Girl. Dr. Laurie was an officer in the nationally based American Academy of School Psychology and Director on the Executive Board of the New York Association of Play Therapy. As a media referral specialist for the American Psychological Association, she has contributed to nearly 200 news stories regarding child development. Dr. Laurie and her psychologist husband, Dr. Fred, are both certified Red Cross Disaster Mental Health volunteers. Happily married for nearly 40 years, they have raised four children and relish their roles as grandparents.

**Dr. Frank (Fred) Zelinger** is a licensed psychologist and certified School District Administrator with over 45 years' professional experience. He has integrated his analytically based Doctoral training from New York University with a variety of life experiences that include raising four sons; working as a school psychologist; running a public elementary school as its Principal; being District Chairperson of the Committee on Special Education; owning and operating several retail establishments; coaching four sports over a period of four decades; consulting in a private religious Day School; enjoying "sixties" music; playing guitar, golf, cards, and racquetball, and maintaining a vibrant and busy private practice as a clinical psychologist. To some degree, Dr. Fred Zelinger credits this diversity of life experience to his ability to understand and develop practical approaches to the needs of his patients. Born in Germany as the first son of concentration camp survivors, his sensitivity to underlying cultural values has a prominent place in the often-short term and pragmatic solutions he helps his diverse clients develop in response to the many issues and concerns that face them in this complicated world. Dr. Fred appreciates the importance of family and supports others in their personal and professional relationships. This, his first book, was a collaborative effort with Laurie, his wife of nearly 40 years. It is based on research as well as firsthand experience, with the hope that other parents can profit from the information they share.

Visit them at www.DrZelinger.com

# Please Explain Anxiety to Me!

This book translates anxiety from the jargon of psychology into concrete experiences that children can relate to. Children and their parents will understand the biological and emotional components of anxiety responsible for the upsetting symptoms they experience. *Please Explain Anxiety to Me, 2nd Edition* gives accurate physiological information in child-friendly language. A colorful dinosaur story explains the link between brain and body functioning, followed by practical therapeutic techniques that children can use to help themselves. Children will:

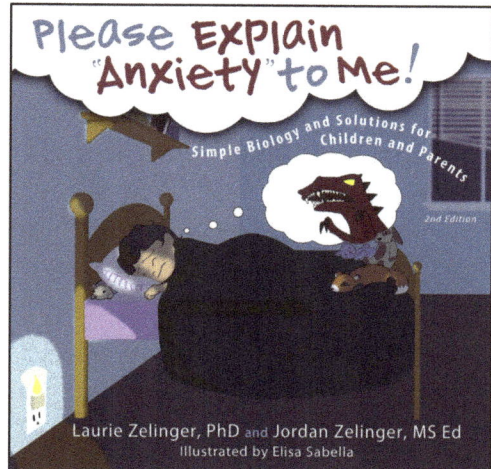

- learn that they can handle most issues if they are explained at their developmental level
- understand the brain/body connection underlying anxiety
- identify with the examples given
- find comfort and reassurance in knowing that others have the same experience
- be provided with strategies and ideas to help them change their anxiety responses
- be able to enjoy childhood and to stop unnecessary worrying

**Therapists and Educators Praise *Please Explain Anxiety To Me, Second Edition***

"On any given day, around thirty percent of my patients have anxiety related symptoms. The simplicity and completeness of the explanations and treatment of anxiety given in this book is remarkable. Defining the cause, treating the core symptoms, and most importantly bringing it to a child's level accompanied by wonderful illustrations, is an incredible feat. I will definitely use this book in my practice."

Zev Ash, M.D. F.A.A.P., Pediatrician

"This excellent book is perfect for parents to read and discuss with their children. It's also perfect for school professionals to use in the school setting."

Herb R. Brown, Ed.D., Superintendent of Schools Oceanside Public Schools, New York

"...A charming--and calming--explanation of anxiety that will help both children and their parents turn their internal worry switches to the OFF position."

Ellen Singer, New York Times-acclaimed bestselling author

Learn more at **www.DrZelinger.com**

ISBN 978-1-61599-216-4

# Please Explain "Terrorism" to Me!
# A Story for Children, P-E-A-R-L-S of Wisdom for their Parents

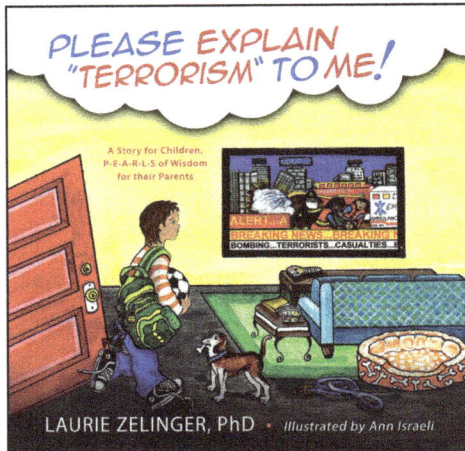

Complemented by exquisite, colorful artwork, Dr. Zelinger skillfully crafts an easily relatable children's story using everyday situations, around the oppressive concept of Terrorism in the news. With masterful understanding of the child's world, new and frightening concepts are introduced carefully and gently, with the child's perspective in mind.

Dr. Zelinger provides parent coaching to further the dialogue in her P-E-A-R-L-S of Wisdom section (Prepare, Explain, Answer, Reassure, Listen, Safeguard) where caregivers are given scripts to guide them, as well room for individuality. This pioneer book helps children and parents face a critical, often avoided topic with reassurance and calm.

"This book provides the 'PEARLS' of wisdom for parents and children to discuss a scary topic like terrorism in ways that promote healthy and authentic parent-child conversations that yield to mutual respect and bonding."

—Marc A. Brackett, Ph.D., Director, Yale Center for Emotional Intelligence

"This fascinating guide amounts to a riveting lesson of clarity and to a masterpiece in bridging the unbridgeable."

—Hon. Yehuda Lancry, Former Ambassador of Israel to the U.N.

"Dr. Zelinger uses common sense, a simple clarification of the basic issues, and reassurance to provide a deeper understanding of terrorism for kids—without a corresponding rise in anxiety."

—Thomas W. Phelan, Ph.D., Psychologist/Author

**Dr. Laurie Zelinger** is a distinguished Board Certified Psychologist with Diplomate status in school psychology as well as a credentialed play therapist who serves on executive boards of state and national organizations. Illustrator Ann Israeli is a retired art teacher, wallpaper and textile designer.

Learn more at **www.DrZelinger.com**

ISBN 978-1-61599-291-1

From Loving Healing Press

## Please Explain Tonsillectomy & Adenoidectomy to Me: A Complete Guide to Preparing Your Child for Surgery, 3rd Edition

Nearly 500,000 adenotonsillectomies will be performed on children this year. Will you be ready?

The new 3rd Edition of this bestselling book helps parents understand and organize the necessary medical and emotional components that accompany their child's surgery. In an easy to follow timeline for events prior to and following a tonsillectomy and/or adenoidectomy, the authors provide reassuring and accurate guidance that eases the process for the patient and family. As caregivers, you will:

- Get the facts about tonsils and adenoids in simple terms.
- Reduce your own anxiety about surgery and recovery.
- Learn how to best support your child through the medical and emotional events surrounding the procedure.
- Have scripts available to guide your conversations with all of your children.
- Discover the sequence of events leading up to surgery and how to prepare for them.
- Find out what you need to have at home while your child recuperates.
- Understand and respond to any unforeseen complications.
- Become confident that you have maximized your child's comfort and adjustment during the weeks surrounding surgery.

"A handy and valuable guide for parents who face the ultimate decision to have their child undergo a surgery, this book unravels the fear, answers the questions and makes it understandable and reassuring. It is much needed in the field and its joyful illustrations make it easy to follow and comprehend."
—Donna Geffner, Ph.D., Ed.D (Hon.), CCC-SP/A,
Past president of the American Speech-Language Hearing Association (ASHA)

"When reading the book, you feel as if Dr. Laurie is right in front of you and leading you through the whole process. This book provides a useful, simple and straight forward approach for parents and children to deal with the anxiety that precedes any surgery."
—Zev Ash, M.D., F.A.A.P. (pediatrician)

Learn more at www.DrZelinger.com

ISBN 978-1-61599-418-2

From Loving Healing Press

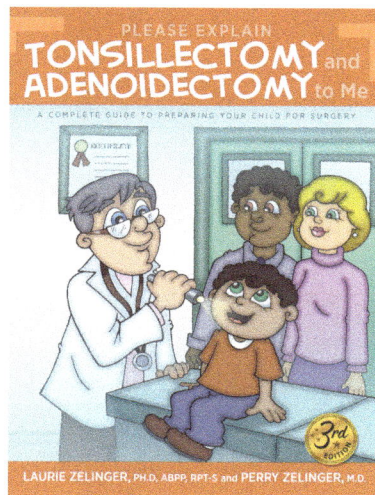

www.ingramcontent.com/pod-product-compliance
Lightning Source LLC
Chambersburg PA
CBHW041426270326
41931CB00023B/3493